GROWTH GUIDE

THIS ISN'T
THE LIFE I
~~*Signed*~~
UP FOR

Bethany House Books
by Donna Partow

Becoming a Vessel God Can Use
Becoming a Vessel God Can Use AudioBook
Becoming a Vessel God Can Use Prayer Journal
Living in Absolute Freedom
Standing Firm
This Isn't the Life I Signed Up For
This Isn't the Life I Signed Up For AudioBook
This Isn't the Life I Signed Up For Growth Guide
Walking in Total God-Confidence
A Woman's Guide to Personality Types

EXTRACTING THE PRECIOUS
2 Corinthians
Isaiah

GROWTH GUIDE

THIS ISN'T THE LIFE I

x̄ *Signed* UP FOR

DONNA PARTOW

BETHANYHOUSE

MINNEAPOLIS, MINNESOTA

Published by Bethany House Publishers
11400 Hampshire Avenue South
Bloomington, Minnesota 55438
www.bethanyhouse.com

Bethany House Publishers is a Division of
Baker Book House Company, Grand Rapids, Michigan.

Printed in the United States of America

Library of Congress Cataloging-in-Publication Data

Partow, Donna.
    Growth guide to accompany This isn't the life I signed up for : —but I'm finding
hope and healing / by Donna Partow.
        p.   cm.
    ISBN 0-7642-2671-1 (pbk.)
    1. Christian women—Religious life. 2. Spiritual life—Christianity. 3. Christian
life—Biblical teaching—Textbooks. 4. Bible—Textbooks. I. Partow, Donna. This isn't
the life I signed up for. II. Title.

BV4527.P373   2003
248.8'43—dc21
                                                                    2002155877

DONNA PARTOW is a Christian communicator with a compelling testimony of God's transforming power. Her uncommon transparency and passion for Christ have been used by God at women's conferences and retreats throughout North America. She is the bestselling author of numerous books and has been a popular guest on more than two hundred radio and TV programs, including *Focus on the Family*.

If your church sponsors an annual women's conference or retreat, perhaps they would be interested in learning more about the author's special weekend programs. She is also available for luncheons and one-day events. For more information, contact:

Donna Partow
Web site: *www.becomingavessel.com*
E-mail: donnapartow@cox.net

ACKNOWLEDGMENTS

I would like to acknowledge the assistance of the following women, who gave valuable insight into both the book and the growth guide you now hold in your hands:

The Apron Gang,
   Vermillion, OH
Eileen Banks
Noreen Boone
Lynn Cheetham
Sandy Cullum
Loreen Desrosiers
Jacque Fewkes
Ann Flaherty
Debby France
Debbie Gilbert
Jeanne Helstrom
Cheryl Jones
Chris Khamlin
Kathy Lee
Deborah Lovett
Pat McBeth
Cindy Measel

Nancy Baccaro
Ginny Bass
Barbara Byrd
Elisa Chung
Dr. Brenda Cusack
Sheila Feltner
Betty Fitch
Lynne Ford
Becky Freeman
Cindy Heflin
Stephanie Janke
Rhoni Kaastra
Vicki J. Kuyper
Judy Link
Suzy Manning
Carolyn McIntyre
Yvonne Ortega

Gail Padilla
Tracie Peterson
Brenda Ponceroff
Lecia Segaard
Connie Smith
Donna Van Buren
Denise Walker
Shari Wiegel
Kendra Brown Wilder

Angela Patton
Melissa Polley
Joanne Richards
Patti Shadbolt
Helen Stellwag
Marjorie Vawter
Lorie Walton
Sabrina White
Trudy Wolcott

My heartfelt thanks to each one of you for your creativity, wisdom, and willingness to "tell it like it is!"

CONTENTS

How to Use This Growth Guide

Reading a book won't necessarily change your life, but *praying through* and *working through* a book most definitely will. If you've picked up this study guide, my guess is that you've already obtained a copy of the book *This Isn't the Life I Signed Up For . . . But I'm Finding Hope and Healing*. If not, I would strongly encourage you to do so. While I believe you can profitably work through the guide without reading the book, you will gain much more from the experience if you use it as it was designed: a companion to supplement your reading.

It is also possible to work through the book and this companion growth guide in your own personal devotional time. However, you will gain far more insight and increase your likelihood of experiencing lasting change if you work through the material with a trusted friend, a small group, or as part of a weekly women's Bible study. There is strength in numbers and power in accountability. If you aren't part of an established group, be bold enough to pick up the phone and make a few calls. No doubt you are surrounded by women who feel trapped in the middle of "the life they didn't sign up for." You may be doing them one of the greatest favors of their lives by inviting them to join you on your journey to hope and healing.

Each week of your journey will include the following components to accompany your reading of the book:

Key Verses

I have selected one or two verses that tie in with the chapter theme. I encourage you to choose one each week to memorize. To facilitate that process, you will find cards at the back of the guide. I encourage you to cut these out and tuck them in your purse. Whenever you have a free moment, pull them out and review them. Also in the back of the book you will find Affirmation cards, or personalized Scripture passages, (as explained in chapter 6). These are designed specifically for daily recitation and should ideally be read aloud.

Key Points to Remember

If you have read the corresponding chapter in *This Isn't the Life I Signed Up For,* these key points will serve to refresh your memory about the most important material covered. If you didn't have an opportunity to read the book itself (perhaps you had a hectic week), these points will serve as your *"Cliffs Notes"* to prepare for your small group time! If you are not reading the book, then the key points will provide an introduction to the concepts and a springboard into the application questions and other activities.

Application Questions

This is the heart of the study. It's your opportunity to reflect upon what you've learned, while learning more about yourself in the process. If you are participating in a group study, it is vital for you to spend time seriously considering the questions posed, as they will form the basis of your group discussion. You owe it to yourself—and to the other women traveling this journey with you—to be fully prepared to contribute to the dialogue. If you are pressed for time in preparing for class, this is the area where you should focus your attention. Although I think you will be robbing yourself of a blessing if you skip the associated chapter reading, I've tried to design the questions so that you CAN answer them just by reviewing the bulleted "Key Points."

Some groups have gone so far as to say, "If you haven't answered the questions *in writing,* we are still glad you came. You can share your prayer requests, enjoy the snack time, listen attentively to what other women have gleaned from the study, and enjoy fellowship with your sisters. However, you are not welcome to join in the study discussion time." This may seem harsh, but it might be just the spur some women need to come prepared. I will leave it up to each group to decide how they want to handle "the unprepared ones"!

Digging Deeper

Okay, this section is for the serious Bible students out there. I would consider this optional but extremely beneficial. Some weeks you may have time to dig deeper—and you'll always be glad you did. But I completely understand that there will probably be other occasions when you may not be able to invest as much time in independent study. Therefore, the material covered in this section will NOT be included in your group discussion. (Did I just hear some of you heave a sigh of relief?)

Working It Into Your Life

Now the proverbial rubber meets the road. In this section of the guide, you'll have the opportunity to put what you are learning into action in the real world. Each chapter will have at least one practical assignment or a suggested step you can take to move closer to experiencing the life you DID sign up for!

Rewrite One of This Week's Key Verses

I truly believe one of the best ways to memorize Scripture is to write it out. This space is provided for you to write (and rewrite if space allows) your favorite verse of the week. Don't leave this space blank! (I have ways of checking up on you.) I would even encourage you to take this process one step further. Purchase Post-it Notes and rewrite the verse again (perhaps multiple times) on these and stick them all over your house—especially in places where you are most likely to be staring into space! (I'll leave it to your imagination to figure out where those places might be.)

Here's a little tip I've mentioned in previous books to which readers have responded well: Write out the first letter of each word in the verse on an index card, Post-it Note, or slip of paper. Walk away for a while, then come back and see if you can fill in the verse using only the first letters as your clues. Don't ask me why, but this really seems to work!

Your Prayer in Response

Space has been provided for you to write out a prayer in response to what God has shown you in your study time. Again, I strongly encourage you to avail yourself of the space provided to practice the vital spiritual discipline of prayer journaling. It is my hope and prayer that you will want to write even more than the space provided allows—and that this study will be a springboard toward full-fledged prayer journaling. That's because prayer journaling is one of the most powerful tools for spiritual cleansing, hearing the voice of God . . . and for finding hope and healing.

If you are in a small group, your leader may ask for volunteers to share their written prayers with the class. This is not a requirement, but I believe it will be a blessing to all involved.

Closing Prayer

For those of you who enjoy guided prayer, I have included a brief prayer to conclude each chapter's study. These are from my heart, and I pray they will bless your heart as well.

So, there you have it: your guide to the growth guide! I pray that this material will move you far along the journey to finding hope and healing. If it makes a difference in your life or in the lives of the women in your group, I would love to hear from you. You can e-mail me at *donnapartow@cox.net* or check out my Web site, *www.becomingavessel.com,* for information on hosting or attending a seminar in your area.

Blessings,
Donna Partow

I Didn't Sign Up for This Life!

This day I call heaven and earth as witnesses against you that I have set before you life and death, blessings and curses. Now choose life, so that you and your children may live and that you may love the Lord your God, listen to his voice, and hold fast to him.

DEUTERONOMY 30:19–20

❀Key Points to Remember

✗ No one signs up for the challenges of life, but in the real world, tough times are inevitable.

✗ When faced with life's heartaches, we have a choice: stay stuck in the place of pain or move forward to find hope and healing.

✗ God sets choices before each of us every day; every moment we are making choices that lead either to life or death.

✗ God could have created a world filled with flawless humans who had no choice but to do the right thing; he chose to give us free will instead.

✗ We are created in the image of God, and I believe he finds more joy in one person who *chooses* to love him— and to keep on loving him even in the face of tragedy— than he finds in all the beauty of every other created thing combined.

✗ This book is about truth, and some of it will be hard to hear. "The truth will set you free, but first it's gonna hurt your feelings."

✗ An easy life isn't necessarily a good life, and a good life is rarely easy.

✗ It's time to let go of the need to be right and start pursuing the need to be healed.

? Application Questions

1. Have you ever felt trapped in the middle of "the life you didn't sign up for"? Perhaps you feel that way now. Describe.

2. What are some of the heartaches and challenges you've faced in your life?

3. In the past, have you chosen to stay stuck in the place of pain? Describe the results.

4. Are you now ready to move forward to find hope and healing? If so, what has motivated you to do so at this time?

5. How do you typically respond when someone tells you something you didn't want to hear?

6. Recall a time in your life when the truth set you free . . . but only after it hurt your feelings.

7. In what ways have you felt as though life has been unfair to you? Why?

8. How have you responded in those times, and do you feel as though God was pleased with your actions?

9. What is your definition of getting real?

10. What keeps you from getting real?

11. What do you hope to accomplish in getting real?

12. What percentage of your suffering is likely the natural consequences of your own choices?

13. If you had to honestly rank your lifelong level of suffering on a scale of 1–10, what number would you choose? (1 = just-about-perfect life; 10 = bankrupt, quadriplegic, sole survivor of a plane crash in the jungles of Ecuador)

Digging Deeper

✗ Read Isaiah 61:1–3:
What does God promise to do for us in times of trials if we trust him?

What will he give us instead of ashes?

Why did he promise this?

In what area of your life do you need to exchange your ashes for beauty?

✘ Read 2 Kings 20:4–5:
What does God hear and see?

What does he promise to do?

✘ Meditate on Psalm 139:
What does God know about you?

Is he surprised by your life circumstances?

What comfort did you find in this psalm? Express your gratitude to the God who made you, loves you, and knows all the days ordained for you.

Look up each of the following verses and note what you discover about hope and/or healing:

Jeremiah 30:17

Jeremiah 33:6

Luke 8:43–48

Proverbs 12:18

Proverbs 13:17–18

Proverbs 15:4

Isaiah 58:6–9

Malachi 4:2

Psalm 25:3–7

Psalm 31:22–24

℘ Working It Into Your Life

Make a list of the top five things you didn't sign up for. Pray over each one and ask God to show you how each one "worked together for good" by teaching you valuable life lessons.

What Happened   Lesson Learned

1. _____   1. _____

2. _____   2. _____

3. _____   3. _____

4. _____   4. _____

5. _____   5. _____

If you are completing this study as part of a small group, gather personal items or photos to represent several of the top ten things you didn't sign up for, and be prepared to briefly describe the lesson you learned or one good thing that came out of the experience.

Review your list and ask God to show you someone who is currently facing a similar challenge. Either call or write that person a note of encouragement, *sharing one Scripture* God used to encourage you.

✎ Rewrite This Week's Key Verse

_____

_____

_____

_____

_____

/ Your Prayer in Response

_____

_____

_____

_____

_____

_____

_____

_____

_____

_____

_____

Heavenly Father, you know this isn't the life I signed up for. There have been heartaches and disappointments along the way—some of them because of my own foolish choices. I ask you now to send the Holy Spirit to do a work of healing in my life. Fill me with hope for a better future. In Jesus' name, amen.

CHAPTER TWO

I Didn't Sign Up for
a Painful Childhood

*When he lies, he speaks his native language, for he is a liar
and the father of lies.*

JOHN 8:44

*If you keep on biting and devouring each other, watch out or
you will be destroyed by each other.*

GALATIANS 5:15

❀Key Points to Remember

✖ Sometimes other people's choices rock our world, because we must reap the consequences of their poor choices. That can leave us feeling powerless.

✖ The sense of powerlessness can lead us to become emotional cannibals.

✖ An emotional cannibal is someone who tries to make herself feel more powerful by "consuming" (or as the Scripture says, "devouring") other people.

✖ Satan acts as the Destructive Seed Planter, planting lies deep in our hearts . . . and he usually comes early to do his dirty work.

✖ Just as God works through people to accomplish his purposes on the earth, so Satan works through human vessels to plant his destructive lies.

✖ Each lie planted in your heart is like a hot button— when people press it, you jump!

✖ If you are routinely angry, offended, or disappointed, you've got lies that need to be uprooted.

✖ Other people's actions toward you say nothing about your worth as a human being. Instead they speak volumes about the brokenness of the one(s) who failed you.

❓ Application Questions

1. What are some of the events that have shaped your life (in particular, your childhood)?

2. What are some of the ways you have screamed to be heard in your life?

3. Are you an emotional cannibal?

4. Can you think of some occasions when you've tried to make yourself feel more powerful by consuming someone else?

5. Have you ever been the victim of emotional cannibalism?

6. What were the results in your life?

7. Have you seen the destructive influence of emotional cannibals in your church? What have been the results?

8. Could you identify with the "cannibal at lunch" scenario? If you were in that scene, which role would you be more likely to fall into? The cannibal . . . or the woman "on the menu"?

9. How hard is it for you to "let it go" when someone hurts your feelings?

10. How likely are you to start "dialing for dollars" and working yourself into an angry snit over some offense?

11. Have you ever allowed someone else's opinion of you to become the centerpiece of your existence?

12. What were some of the destructive lies planted in your heart?

13. Do you know who planted them?

14. What has been the result of believing those lies?

15. What lies have YOU unwittingly planted in the lives of your own children?

16. What steps do you need to take to undo the damage done?

Digging Deeper

✗ Read Matthew 15:16–19:
What sins does Jesus specifically mention?

Were you surprised to find slander listed among the other sins we might consider far more serious?

How does that make you feel about your involvement with slander?

Look up slander in the dictionary. Write the definition below.

Have you been guilty of slandering someone? Who?

What steps do you need to take to make things right?

✗ Read 1 Peter 5:6–10:
What two character qualities are mentioned in verse 8?

How can these prepare us to stand firm in the face of attacks?

How should we respond when the devil tries to devour us (perhaps sending a human vessel to do the job)?

✘ Read Psalm 27:10:
Who does this passage say may forsake you?

What does the inclusion of this passage imply about the relationship between some parents and their children?

Who does this passage assure us will never forsake us?

✘ Meditate on Psalm 86:
Who does the psalmist want to "hear" him?

Do you tell your problems to God . . . or to everyone else?

What does the psalmist ask God to do for him?

List some of God's character qualities mentioned in the psalm.

How can knowing who God is help you recover from the pain/power of destructive seeds?

It is not enough to uproot lies. We have to replace them with the truth. Be sure to fill your mind with God's truth and his promises that apply to your specific area of need so that the vacancy left by uprooted lies can be filled with truth, rather than a new set of lies. Look up the following passages and note what truths you discover about your identity and the basis of your security:

Deuteronomy 33:12

Isaiah 43:4

Isaiah 49:16

Isaiah 54:9–10

Romans 8:14–17

Romans 8:38–39

1 Thessalonians 1:4

Ephesians 4:24

1 Peter 2:9–10

1 John 3:1

Working It Into Your Life

List five lies that were planted in your heart, along with the person who planted them. If you are concerned about confidentiality, you can write your answer on a separate piece of paper and destroy it after your "surgery."

Lie   Seed Planter

1. _____   1. _____

2. _____   2. _____

3. _____   3. _____

4. _____   4. _____

5. _____   5. _____

Set aside time for the Holy Spirit to uproot those lies. Pray and grieve over each one. You might adapt the following prayer:

> I'm not going to believe destructive lies—not one more day. I refuse to let this defeat me. I've wasted enough years allowing the pain of my childhood to control me. The people who hurt me have no right to determine my destiny. They don't deserve that much power over my life. I'm not going to let them rent space in my head anymore. I am hereby serving them—and the enemy—with eviction notices. Get out! And while I'm at it, I'm going to close the door to the enemy by choosing to forgive the people who hurt me most. I know they inflicted pain because they were in pain.

Now, ask God to show you the brokenness of each seed planter. Take out photos of that person if you have them available and seek to see that person with new eyes—God's eyes.

Seed Planter	Source of His/Her Brokenness
1. _____	1. _____
2. _____	2. _____
3. _____	3. _____
4. _____	4. _____
5. _____	5. _____

If you can find the strength to do so, you will find it incredibly healing to actually pray for the ones who have caused you pain. You might pray specifically that God will help them overcome the source of their brokenness and the lies that were planted in their hearts. I know, from personal experience, how hard this is. I also know, ultimately, how healing it is.

If you are part of a small group, bring photos from your childhood and your yearbook (or other symbols of the seed planters in your life) with you to class.

✎ Rewrite One of This Week's Key Verses

_____

_____

_____

_____

_____

_____

✐ Your Prayer in Response

_____

_____

_____

_____

_____

_____

_____

_____

_____

_____

Heavenly Father, thank you for sending your Holy Spirit to lead me into all truth. I thank you for the words of your Son, Jesus, who said I WILL know the truth and it will set me free. Help me to break free from the power of lies and begin to walk in the power of truth. Help me to forgive others, just as you, through Christ, forgave me. Amen.

CHAPTER THREE

I Didn't Sign Up for Disappointing Relationships

For if you forgive men when they sin against you, your heavenly Father will also forgive you. But if you do not forgive men their sins, your Father will not forgive your sins.

MATTHEW 6:14–15

See to it that no one misses the grace of God and that no bitter root grows up to cause trouble and defile many.

HEBREWS 12:15

❋Key Points to Remember

- ✘ Just as God works through human vessels to accomplish his purposes on the earth, the enemy does also.

- ✘ Because we are all fragile jars of clay, it's inevitable that we will disappoint one another on a routine basis.

- ✘ Forgiveness is the most precious gift—and the most powerful tool—God has given us.

- ✘ When we extend forgiveness, we are closer to the heart of God than at any other time.

- ✘ The more gracious we are, the more inclined people are to be gracious toward us.

- ✘ No one signs up to be "wronged," but until we forgive those who hurt us, we are signing up daily to let the enemy have a field day with our lives.

- ✘ Those who hurt you were most certainly victims before they became victimizers.

- ✘ Bitterness is like a contagious disease: first it spreads throughout our own body; then it begins to overtake the people around us.

- ✘ One way to deal with resentment is to acknowledge the suffering of the other person.

- ✘ Forgiveness involves letting go of a precious story we tell about ourselves, risking the awareness of a larger, less self-justifying truth.

? Application Questions

1. Recall some of the disappointing relationships in your life. Why were they a disappointment?

2. In what way did you "set yourself up" for disappointment by having unrealistic expectations?

3. Recall a time when you were a disappointment to others. Why did it happen?

4. How would you handle the situation differently if you had it to do all over again?

5. Do you consider yourself a forgiving—or unforgiving—person?

6. To test yourself: are people quick to forgive you? If not, is it possible the reason is that you are *not* a forgiving person?

7. Recall the woman who had been divorced twenty-two years but was trapped in the pain. Then, as you consider the condition of your health and your family, is there any possibility that your unforgiveness is part of the problem?

8. Is there a person in your life to whom you invariably speak in a "certain tone of voice"?

9. What deep-seated bitterness might be causing your negative attitude?

10. One way to deal with resentment is to acknowledge the suffering of the other person. In detail, in writing, acknowledge the pain of each person who has hurt you. (Walk a mile in their shoes.)

11. Has anyone ever pressured you to "sweep it under the carpet" rather than letting you deal with your pain?

12. What was the result?

13. As you think of the person who has hurt you most, what is your response to the following question: What if God's judgment is to grant that person the same forgiveness you were granted at the foot of the cross?

☞Digging Deeper

✗ Read Genesis 50:15–21:
Why do you think Joseph wept when he received the message from his brothers?

What is the significance of Joseph's rhetorical question in verse 19?

How can you apply his perspective in verse 20 to your daily experience?

✘ Meditate on Psalm 25:
In what ways can the pain of your past be likened unto "enemies"?

Who will never be put to shame?

What does the psalmist ask God to show him?

What does the psalmist ask God to do for him?

What does the psalmist reveal about who God is and what he does?

Studying the following passages, what do you learn about resentment and forgiveness?

Ephesians 4:31–32

Matthew 18:21–35

Mark 11:25

Colossians 3:12–14

Hebrews 12:14–15

2 Corinthians 2:6–11

James 3:2

Romans 2:1–4

Working It Into Your Life

1. Relationship Survey: On a scale from 1 to 10, rate your contentment with each of the following relationships (with 1 being extremely disappointed and 10 being blissfully happy):

_____ Parents
_____ Siblings
_____ Spouse
_____ Children
_____ Co-workers
_____ Neighbors
_____ Old friends
_____ New friends
_____ Acquaintances

Now go back and evaluate how you might overcome disappointment in each of these relationships, and ask God to show you if part of the problem is your own unrealistic expectations. You might also write out a description of realistic expectations for each relationship.

2. Reread the description of the courtroom scene in chapter 3 of *This Isn't the Life I Signed Up For*. Ask God to show you (although you probably already know) which person in your life you are most in need of forgiving. On a separate sheet of paper, make a list detailing exactly what that person has done and what his or her sin has cost you (e.g., lost opportunities for other relationships, inability to trust, physical ailments rooted in emotional turmoil, lost sleep, broken friendships, etc.).

Now walk into the courtroom and begin advocating your case. In your own mind, picture God stepping into the courtroom . . . and picture yourself giving God the list.

Next, rewrite as many times as you need to:
"Father, forgive _____, for he (or she) did not know what he (or she) was doing."

✎ Rewrite One of This Week's Key Verses

_____

_____

_____

_____

_____

_____

✎ Your Prayer in Response

_____

_____

_____

_____

_____

_____

_____

_____

_____

_____

Heavenly Father, thank you for the incredible gift of forgiveness. I know it is the road that led me back to your house because Jesus paved the way. Now let me experience forgiveness as the road to healing, as I forgive those who have sinned against me. Holy Spirit, lead me into the full truth about those who have hurt me. Give me new eyes to see them not as those who have hurt me but as people who have been broken by the world. In Jesus' name, amen.

CHAPTER FOUR

I Didn't Sign Up to Make Foolish Choices

Do not judge, or you too will be judged. For in the same way you judge others, you will be judged, and with the measure you use, it will be measured to you.

MATTHEW 7:1–2

But you are a chosen people, a royal priesthood, a holy nation, a people belonging to God, that you may declare the praises of him who called you out of darkness into his wonderful light. Once you were not a people, but now you are the people of God; once you had not received mercy, but now you have received mercy.

1 PETER 2:9–10

❀Key Points to Remember

✘ One of the reasons we face so many tests is because we pass so many judgments.

✘ God warns us in advance what will happen when we judge others or violate any of the other fundamental laws of the universe (such as, you reap what you sow).

✘ When we judge another person, we are putting ourselves in the place of God and we set in motion powerful spiritual forces. It's like whistling for the devil and inviting him to tempt us with the same test we judged others for being unable to withstand.

✘ Some of us need to make the painful admission that our lives are not where God wants them to be; they are where our own foolish choices have brought us.

✘ This may not be the life you deliberately signed up for, but if you are honest, it may very well be the logical outcome of your life choices . . . and the choices of those around you.

✘ No matter how hard you try, you cannot make disobedience look like obedience!

✘ God never promotes disobedience, and he never places his children in spiritually compromising positions. We do that on our own.

✘ Your circumstances are not the only measure of your obedience, but sometimes they do reveal your disobedience in the form of "bleating sheep." (Bleating sheep are the negative logical consequences of your choices and the choices of those closest to you.)

✘ Sometimes we believe God will be so pleased with our sacrifices, he will overlook our disobedience. But the Scripture says, "To obey is better than sacrifice."

? Application Questions

1. Do you ever feel like God is picking on you? Describe.

2. Does the universe seem like a terribly unjust, confusing place? Why?

3. Have you ever noted a connection between the number of judgments you pass and the number of trials you face? Do you think there is a connection?

4. Are you a judgmental person? Go get a second (and third) opinion before you answer!

5. In what way have you been "getting back what you've been giving the world"?

6. Can you think of a specific judgment that came back at you? Were you "blindsided" when the test came?

7. List below the major tests you've faced in life. Now think back. Have you ever judged someone for how they handled that same test? Make the connection!

8. Do you know what it feels like to be "the unpicked one"? Recall a circumstance when you felt that way.

9. If you are honest, is it possible your life is NOT where God wants it to be . . . it's where your own foolish choices have brought you? What were those choices?

10. Have you ever felt like the woman in the scene from *Out of Africa*? Have you ever knelt before God and said, "All gone"? Do you need to do that right now?

11. Could you identify in any way with Donna's story about the two trips to the river? In what way?

12. Is there an area of your life where you have previously claimed to be "suffering for Jesus" but you now realize you are simply suffering for your own foolish choices?

13. Are there any "bleating sheep" in your life?

14. Is there an area in your life where your circumstances contradict your claims?

15. Is there an area in your life where you have tried to substitute sacrifice for obedience?

16. How did you respond to the story of Bea and the overturned trash can? Are you in some way trying to "prolong your punishment" rather than enjoying God's mercy?

Digging Deeper

✕ Read Romans 2:1–4:
What does this passage say about people who pass judgment?

How do we show contempt for God's kindness?

What is the connection between passing judgment and showing contempt toward God?

✗ Meditate on Psalm 119:1–48:
What does the psalmist commit himself to?

What does he ask God to do for him?

What do you learn from this passage about "our part" and "God's part" in avoiding foolish choices?

Look up the following verses and note what you observe about sowing and reaping:

Hosea 8:7

Hosea 10:12

James 2:1–4

James 2:12–13

James 3:18

Psalm 126:5–6

Ecclesiastes 11:6

Proverbs 11:18

2 Corinthians 9:6–11

Galatians 6:7–10

☺ Working It Into Your Life

1. Make a conscious effort to listen to yourself this week. Every time you catch yourself saying or thinking phrases like "I would NEVER" or "I can't believe she" or "How could you," write it down. Ask the Lord to make you aware of the judgments you routinely pass. Meanwhile, recall times you have used those phrases, and complete each sentence below with some typical words you might say:

Oh, I can't believe _____

_____

How could you _____

_____

I would NEVER _____

_____

2. Spend some time in prayer, asking God to show you any "bleating sheep" in your life. (Remember: bleating sheep are the logical negative consequences of your choices.) Be ruthlessly honest. List some of your sheep:

_____   _____

_____   _____

_____   _____

_____   _____

3. If you have a large herd of sheep, go buy yourself a stuffed sheep and keep it in your prayer room as a reminder that your choices have consequences!

4. If you are part of a group, bring your stuffed sheep to class with you and be prepared to talk about one of the "bleating sheep" God revealed to you.

✎ Rewrite One of This Week's Key Verses

_____

_____

_____

_____

_____

_____

✎ Your Prayer in Response

_____

_____

_____

_____

_____

_____

_____

_____

_____

_____

Heavenly Father, I am grateful that you have designed a universe that makes sense. In the past, my life has seemed so chaotic and incomprehensible to me. I thank you for sending your Holy Spirit this week to show me the principle of sowing and reaping. I'm grateful for the knowledge that as I begin to sow differently, I will begin to reap differently. Thank you that Jesus came so that I can have an abundant life instead of a life filled with bleating sheep! Amen.

CHAPTER FIVE

I Didn't Sign Up for Disappointment With God

His divine power has given us everything we need for life and godliness through our knowledge of him who called us by his own glory and goodness. Through these he has given us his very great and precious promises, so that through them you may participate in the divine nature and escape the corruption in the world caused by evil desires.

2 PETER 1:3–4

Now to him who is able to do immeasurably more than all we ask or imagine, according to his power that is at work within us, to him be glory in the church and in Christ Jesus throughout all generations, for ever and ever! Amen.

EPHESIANS 3:20–21

❀Key Points to Remember

- ✖ Many people are afraid to risk disappointment with God, so they play the game of "low expectations" (expecting very little from God).

- ✖ God chooses to act in response to our faith-filled prayers. To a large extent, your Christian walk is a reflection of what you are asking God for.

- ✖ If you don't believe God will answer your prayers, you have limited him by your unbelief.

- ✖ God wants to bless us *so that* we can be a blessing to others.

- ✖ God's Word is the bread of life . . . not the chewing gum of life!

- ✖ We will reign with God throughout all eternity; our place in the coming kingdom will be determined by our faithfulness here on earth.

- ✖ Every time we do the bare minimum or try to "get away with something" we are robbing ourselves.

- ✖ No matter how disappointing our life has been thus far, we must remain sure of what we hope for and certain of what we do not see.

- ✖ The best way to build our character is in meditation upon the promises of God, convincing our hearts of his goodness.

? Application Questions

1. Do you play the game of "low expectations" with God to protect yourself from being disappointed?

2. Is it possible that the reason you are disappointed with God is because you rarely ask him to do anything incredibly wonderful for you?

3. In what area of your life have you possibly limited God by your unbelief?

4. Have you ever asked for something with the wrong motives behind it? What was the result?

5. Can you handle it when God says no, or are you inclined to fall apart?

6. Has God ever given you something twice? What impact did that have on your life?

7. What has been your approach to spiritual growth: chewing gum or bread?

8. Have you ever fallen into bibliolatry: worshipping the Bible rather than God? Have you reduced God to the object of your investigation, so that your Christian life becomes a list of rules you live by and a set of beliefs you give mental assent to?

9. Do you tend to emphasize the Word or the Spirit? Have you ever gotten out of balance? What was the result?

10. Have you observed the dangers of imbalance in other believers? What were the results?

11. Reread the message on the scroll. What is your reaction?

12. Is the coming kingdom a compelling reality in your life? Or do you try to see "how much you can get away with and still sneak into heaven"?

13. What have you experienced in life that was truly tragic?

14. How did you respond to it initially?

15. Did your response change over time? How?

16. Do you believe tragedy makes people stronger . . . or merely brings out what's already there?

✐ Digging Deeper

✘ Read Genesis 12:1–3:
What did God ask Abraham to do?

What does God promise to do for Abraham in return for this act of faith?

What does this passage tell you about the rewards for "risks of faith"?

✘ Read Habakkuk 3:17–19:
What circumstances were these people facing?

What does this verse tell us about trusting God when life disappoints us?

What does this verse say God will do for those who keep the faith?

✗ Read 2 Samuel 22:20–37:
What does this passage tell you about the character of God?

What has God promised to do for those who live uprightly?

✗ Meditate on Psalm 16:
What can you have apart from the Lord?

What has God done/promised to do for us?

What should our response be?

Look up the following verses and note what you learn about faith:

Matthew 6:28–34

Matthew 8:5–12

Matthew 9:27–31

Matthew 13:58

Matthew 17:17–21

Matthew 21:19–22

Mark 6:4–5

Mark 11:22–25

John 14:11–14

Acts 3:16

🐑 Working It Into Your Life

1. Choose a passage of Scripture you would like to meditate on. Proverbs 4, especially verses 20–22, is a good start, but feel free to select any passage that ministers to where you are right now. Write out the passage on an index card or sheet of paper. However, rephrase and personalize it. For example, change "My son, pay attention to what I say" to "Father, I desire to pay attention to your words." Develop the habit of personalizing Scripture; it will greatly enhance your devotional life. Find a quiet place to sit, and begin to read

and reread the passage, word by word. Think about every word, every sentence. Be still and open your heart to whatever God wants to show you through this passage. Allow at least thirty minutes for this exercise. If you wish, have your prayer journal on hand to write out anything that comes to mind. However, this is primarily an exercise not in prayer journaling but in meditating.

2. Research some of the people mentioned in the Great Hall of Faith. Choose one who is particularly inspiring to you in your life journey right now. If you are part of a small group, be prepared to discuss who you chose and why.

✒ Rewrite One of This Week's Key Verses

_____

_____

_____

_____

_____

✒ Your Prayer in Response

_____

_____

_____

_____

_____

_____

_____

_____

_____

_____

_____

_____

Heavenly Father, thank you for the gift of faith. I ask that, through the leading of the Holy Spirit and my diligent determination to heed his voice, I will begin to grow in my faith. I am so thankful for the teachings of Jesus, who demonstrated so clearly what faith looks like and what it can accomplish. Help me to believe that faith can have the same power in my life as it had in New Testament times. My heart's desire is to walk by faith. Amen.

CHAPTER SIX

I Signed Up for Happiness

Come to me, all you who are weary and burdened, and I will give you rest. Take my yoke upon you and learn from me, for I am gentle and humble in heart, and you will find rest for your souls. For my yoke is easy and my burden is light.

MATTHEW 11:28–30

Do everything without complaining or arguing, so that you may become blameless and pure, children of God without fault in a crooked and depraved generation, in which you shine like stars in the universe as you hold out the word of life—in order that I may boast on the day of Christ that I did not run or labor for nothing.

PHILIPPIANS 2:14–16

✿Key Points to Remember

✗ The problem with carrying heavy loads is that, eventually, you've got to set them down somewhere. Everybody has her own bag of rocks to carry. We have no right to ask someone else to carry ours as well.

✗ Jesus told us to lay our burdens down at his feet, to make it easier for us to resist the temptation to lay them down at everyone else's door.

✗ Most people are pretty much as happy as they've made up their minds to be.

✗ Our experience of the world largely depends on what we choose to focus on: we can focus on what's wrong with the world and be miserable. Or we can focus on what's right with the world and be happy.

✗ When we choose to magnify the bad, it appears larger than it really is. But when we choose to magnify God, we begin to get a clearer picture of reality.

✗ When we choose to magnify God, we remind ourselves that God is larger than all of our problems.

✗ With confidence in God's goodness, we can approach life in a healthy, balanced way that acknowledges the heartaches and disappointments of life but still chooses to see God's redemptive power at work.

✗ Complaining is the opposite of magnifying God. It's like whistling for the devil.

✗ Each of us has an emotional thermostat, which was set at a very young age. We subconsciously work to re-create the temperature that feels most familiar.

? Application Questions

1. Do you feel compelled to run around like a busy little creature? Does it make you feel important? Do you feel unimportant if you are not busy?

2. Do you work yourself to death for your King? How does it affect your relationship with him? How does it affect your happiness?

3. Do you carry around heavy loads . . . and routinely set them down at other people's doors?

4. In what way do you ask other people to carry your bag of rocks in addition to their own?

5. Is there one person in particular you like to complain to? How do you think that affects your relationship?

6. Do you know someone like Cindy—someone with every reason to complain but who keeps a great attitude in the midst of a deep trial? Describe.

7. How has this person's positive attitude affected you and the people around her/him?

8. How would this person's influence be different if he/she constantly complained about the situation?

9. Do you tend to focus on what's right with the world . . . or what's wrong with it? In other words, where do you direct your magnifying glass?

10. What is the result of focusing your attention as you do?

11. How has your complaining affected people around you who were trying to keep a good attitude?

12. How did you react to the statement "complaining is like whistling for the devil"? Explain.

13. What temperature is your emotional thermostat set at? Explain.

14. Do you ever "heat things up" in your life when things get too peaceful?

15. Alternatively, do you panic when things naturally heat up and seek to "lower the temperature" no matter the cost?

✐ Digging Deeper

✗ Read Psalm 1:1–6:
Describe the lifestyle of one who is blessed:

Contrast the lifestyle of the wicked:

What are the benefits enjoyed by the one who is blessed by God?

✗ Meditate on Psalm 34:
List all the things the psalmist "magnifies" about God:

Look up the following Scriptures and note what you discover about happiness and/or things we should be happy for. (Some translations render "happy" as "blessed." If you are so inclined, look up both words in a dictionary.)

Ecclesiastes 2:24–26

Psalm 32:1–2

Psalm 94:12

Proverbs 3:13–18

Proverbs 8:34–36

Proverbs 16:20

Luke 1:45

James 1:12

Revelation 1:3

Working It Into Your Life

1. Locate a magnifying glass and put it in your prayer room as a visual reminder that we can choose, each day, what we will magnify.

2. Buy one of those "fuzzy posters" and color some areas dark, others bright. Or create your own drawing featuring light and dark contrasts. If you are part of a weekly small group, bring your artwork to class.

3. Keep an eye on your "emotional thermostat" this week.

4. Read the affirmations found in the back of this *Growth Guide*. Cut out the ones that help you, or write some of your own. Keep them where you'll see them frequently and begin the habit of reading them daily.

5. Write a list of ten things you have to be thankful about and recite them daily!

_____   _____

_____   _____

_____   _____

_____   _____

_____   _____

✏ Rewrite One of This Week's Key Verses

_____

_____

_____

_____

_____

✏ Your Prayer in Response

_____

_____

_____

_____

_____

_____

_____

Heavenly Father, I thank you for the truth that I can be as happy as I choose to be. You have blessed me in every conceivable way, most of all by sending your Son to die on a cross for me. Above all the "things" I ask for in prayer, all the "things" I think I need to make me happy, Lord, I ask right now for a thankful heart. In Jesus' name, amen.

I Signed Up for Great Health

Jesus went through all the towns and villages, teaching in their synagogues, preaching the good news of the kingdom and healing every disease and sickness.

MATTHEW 9:35

Since we have these promises, dear friends, let us purify ourselves from everything that contaminates body and spirit, perfecting holiness out of reverence for God.

2 CORINTHIANS 7:1

❀Key Points to Remember

✘ Some Christians believe that suffering is inherently noble. As a result, they sometimes passively accept suffering that God never intended them to endure.

✘ It is clear from the book of Job that Satan has the power to afflict people with sickness . . . and God lets him do it. Nevertheless, the lives of God's favored children throughout the Old Testament were characterized by health and long life.

✘ Sometimes chronic illness draws us closer to God, but in many cases it causes people to become self-consumed.

✘ Jesus frequently healed sick people. He didn't go around making people sick so they could prove how much faith they had or to get their attention.

✘ Lack of faith is not the only explanation for the heartaches of life. It definitely explains some things . . . but not all.

✘ The healthiest attitude toward sickness is to view it chiefly as the result of living in a fallen world, not primarily as being sent to us by God to make us holy nor as a result of a lack of faith on our part.

✘ In many instances, sickness is nothing more than the logical consequence of our lifestyle. We don't always need to look for profound supernatural explanations when plain old common sense will do.

✘ Medical science continues to confirm that many illnesses are rooted in emotional pain, which manifests itself in physical pain.

✘ God created us as triune beings: spirit, soul (mind, will, and emotions), and body. Whatever impacts one part of our being impacts the other two parts as well. If we neglect any area, the other two invariably suffer.

✘ The Bible says that meditating on God's Word can literally bring healing to our bodies.

? Application Questions

1. Do you believe suffering is inherently noble? A sign that the sick person is a giant of the faith?

2. Have you ever been guilty of "playing the martyr"? Describe the impact on those around you.

3. In your personal experience, has sickness drawn you closer to God? Or has it made you more self-consumed?

4. In your observation of those around you, which response is most common among sick people (especially those who are chronically sick)?

5. Do you believe God inflicts or allows sickness to "get someone's attention"?

6. How much sickness, in your observation of family and friends, is nothing more than the logical consequences of lifestyle choices?

7. Many Christians neglect their body, then blame God or the devil when they get sick. Have you ever been guilty of doing that?

8. Have you been praying for healing . . . while refusing to make the necessary lifestyle changes that would promote healing?

9. Do you know other people who have done that . . . or perhaps routinely do that?

10. Is it possible that some of your physical suffering is rooted in emotional pain?

11. Again, just from your own personal observation, how much physical suffering do you believe is rooted in emotional pain? Cite examples.

12. On a scale of 1 to 10, how well do you take care of your:

_____ Spirit

_____ Soul

_____ Body

13. Reread the extended passage from *Come Away, My Beloved*. What is your response?

14. Describe your own personal pathway to great health.

✍ Digging Deeper

✗ Read Psalm 6:
What does the psalmist tell us about the health of his soul?

What does he tell us about the health of his body?

What can you discern about the spiritual condition of the psalmist?

What connections can you make between the health of his spirit, soul, and body?

✗ Meditate on Psalm 31:
What do you discover about the circumstances the psalmist is facing?

How does he feel about those circumstances?

What do you discover about the condition of his spirit?

How about his body?

What does he tell us about the condition of his soul?

Again, what conclusions can you draw about the connections between spirit, soul, and body?

How do people treat him?

What does God do for him?

Do you really believe God will do those same things for you?

How does your life (especially the condition of your spirit, soul, and body) give evidence of your belief?

Look up the following verses and note what you discover about health and healing:

Proverbs 3:7–8

Proverbs 4:20–22

Proverbs 12:18

Proverbs 15:4

Proverbs 15:30

Proverbs 16:24

Matthew 4:23

Matthew 9:35

Luke 6:19

Luke 9:10–11

3 John 1:2

Romans 12:1

♡ Working It Into Your Life

1. Carefully evaluate the health of your body, soul, and spirit. Prayerfully consider whether you need to undertake a new diet or fitness regimen.

2. Go to a health food store and explore homeopathic remedies for some of your common ailments.

3. If you are chronically ill, or just feeling sluggish, you might consider undertaking routine fasts to benefit your body and spirit. Begin with a twenty-four-hour fast, then a forty-eight-hour one, and perhaps build up to fasts of three, four, or even seven days. I once met a woman who fasted for forty days! Although I have not lost weight using the forty-eight-hour "diet juices," I have found them extremely beneficial during fasting—they prevent many of the common side effects like headaches and jitters.

✎ Rewrite One of This Week's Key Verses

_____

_____

_____

_____

_____

_____

✎ Your Prayer in Response

_____

_____

_____

_____

_____

_____

_____

_____

_____

_____

Heavenly Father, I know my health is a precious gift

from you. Please forgive me for treating the temple of the

Holy Spirit like a trash can! I know my body is the only

living sacrifice I have to offer you, so I offer it to you right now. Empower me to actively purify my life of anything that contaminates my spirit, soul, or body, so that I can glorify you. In Jesus' name, amen.

CHAPTER EIGHT

I Signed Up for Love

For you created my inmost being;
you knit me together in my mother's womb.
I praise you because I am fearfully and wonderfully made;
your works are wonderful,
I know that full well.
My frame was not hidden from you
when I was made in the secret place.
When I was woven together in the depths of the earth,
your eyes saw my unformed body.

PSALM 139:13–16

My people have committed two sins: They have forsaken me,
the spring of living water, and have dug their own cisterns,
broken cisterns that cannot hold water.

JEREMIAH 2:13

❀Key Points to Remember

- ✗ God wants us to take reasonable care of our bodies, but the obsessive pursuit of perfection is not reasonable—and it will never bring us the love we desire.

- ✗ God says you are lovable exactly the way you are; you don't have to change a thing to earn his love and attention.

- ✗ God designed all of us with a hole in our hearts the size of the Grand Canyon so we would be driven to him to fill us. Unfortunately, we run everywhere else to be filled—and turn into Da Bucket Lady in the process.

- ✗ We go out into the world with our little bucket and expect people to fill us, fix us, love us, make us feel okay. We fail to realize it is impossible to fill a hole the size of the Grand Canyon with a bucket.

- ✗ You can determine who you expect to fill you by asking yourself: Who can make me angrier than anyone else? Who can disappoint me most profoundly? Who do I like to brag about?

- ✗ Many men figure out before their wives do that they will never be able to fill that empty place inside of the women they love . . . so they put down the "bucket" and pick up the remote!

- ✗ The Bible tells us that after the Samaritan woman allowed Jesus to give her the Living Water, she left her bucket at the well. She didn't have to be a Bucket Lady anymore.

- ✗ When you allow the Living Water to fill those empty places in your heart, you won't have to be a Bucket Lady anymore either.

✘ Once you've surrendered your bucket, you can be one of those rare gems who has something genuinely worthwhile to offer the world. You'll have the love of God shed abroad in your heart, overflowing toward everyone you meet.

? Application Questions

1. How do you feel about your body?

2. Is there one part of your body that drives you nuts? What is it? To what lengths have you gone to try to change it?

3. Have you been through a "midlife crisis"? What's the craziest thing you did as a result?

4. Do you take reasonable care of your body?

5. Are you now—or have you ever been—obsessed with the pursuit of perfection? What were the results?

6. Have you ever felt desperate to win male attention? What did that desperation drive you to do?

7. Which kind of love are you seeking?

8. What type of love is most meaningful in your life right now? Who provides that love? Describe.

9. Have you ever sensed God seeking you? When? What was your response?

10. Are you Da Bucket Lady? Who do you expect to bail for you?

11. How has that affected your relationship?

12. How would your relationship be different if you "released your bailer"?

☞ Digging Deeper

✘ Read John 15:9–17:
This was the last opportunity Jesus had to teach his disciples in depth. What subject did he choose to speak about?

What does that tell you about how important this subject is to Jesus?

WHY does he want us to love one another? What will be the result in our own lives when we love others?

✗ Read Ephesians 3:14–21:
List all the things Paul prayed for his friends:

What are we to be rooted and established in?

If you were instructing someone, based on this passage, how to be filled with love, what would you say?

✗ Meditate on Psalm 16, especially verses 9–11:
Who fills the psalmist?

What is he filled with?

How does that filling affect his heart?

How does that filling affect his tongue?

How does it affect his body?

Look up the following Scriptures and note what you discover about love and what we are to be filled with:

John 1:15–16

John 13:34

John 15:9–17

Romans 5:5

Romans 12:9–10

Romans 13:8–10

1 Corinthians 2:9–10

1 Corinthians 13:1–13

1 Peter 1:22

1 John 4:7–12

1 John 4:16–21

⑨ Working It Into Your Life

1. Write love letters to important people in your life: husband, parents, children, friends.

2. Have your own Bucket Surrendering Ceremony as described in the book.

3. Hold a retirement ceremony for your bailer. Take that person out for (or prepare) a special dinner and present him or her with a gift to symbolize the retirement.

✎ Rewrite One of This Week's Key Verses

_____

_____

_____

_____

✎ Your Prayer in Response

_____

_____

_____

_____

_____

_____

_____

Heavenly Father, I thank you for loving me so much you sent your only Son to die on a cross for me. I pray that the Holy Spirit would so fill my heart with love that I would have something to give to others. Help me, Lord, not to be a Bucket Lady—one who desperately seeks love and approval from others. Help me instead to be filled with joy in your presence. Jesus, thank you for showing us how to love and for setting an example by laying down your life. I want to learn to lay my life—my needs and concerns—down so that I can focus on the needs and concerns of others. Amen.

CHAPTER NINE

I Signed Up for the Perfect Little Family

Blessed is the [woman] who fears the Lord,
who finds great delight in his commands.
[Her] children will be mighty in the land;
the generation of the upright will be blessed.

PSALM 112:1–2

❀Key Points to Remember

- ✗ Most Christian books on family life promise that A+B=C; that is, if you do certain things, you are guaranteed certain results. However, some people do A+B but get an F anyway.

- ✗ When you face a family crisis, focus on keeping your heart right before God, and let him handle your circumstances.

- ✗ Don't worry about what the neighbors say about your family; fix your eyes on Jesus and let him transform you from the inside out.

- ✗ When we are more interested in what the neighbors think than what God thinks, we push and shove our families around, trying to fit them into a particular mold.

- ✗ It's not what the neighbors *think* is true about your family that matters; it's what your children *know* is true about your family that matters.

- ✗ God knows our motives, and he will reward us according to what is in our heart, not based upon how well we perform. Live your life before an "Audience of One."

- ✗ Most women define their success according to their relationships: if their husband is successful and their children accomplish a lot, they feel successful. Otherwise, they feel like failures.

- ✗ God's blessing is not for sale and it can't be obtained through working a formula. It is a gift he gives to our children as a reward for our obedience.

? Application Questions

1. Have you ever missed an important event in your child's life? How did that make you feel?

2. Before you had children, no doubt you dreamed of the perfect little family. Describe what you had in mind.

3. How does the reality compare with your dream?

4. Do you notice a disparity between the way Christian family experts say your life "should" be and the way it really is? How do you account for that?

5. Are you among the 70% of the population affected by divorce? How has it affected you?

6. Have you ever faced a family crisis that taught you who your real friends were? What did you learn from that experience?

7. Are you more focused on outward performance or inward reality? What evidence can you give to support your answer?

8. Have you ever been guilty of pushing and shoving your family into a particular mold in an effort to impress other people?

9. Could you relate to the Sunday morning skit?

10. Is there any aspect of your approach to the Christian life that might be driving your children away from church? If so, what changes do you need to make?

11. What did you think of the quote "The last temptation is the final treason: to do the right thing for the wrong reason"? Are you guilty?

12. What is your reaction to the quote "The Cold War is over . . . and the East Germans won"? Do you agree that Americans are pushing their children too hard in sports and many other areas?

13. Do you push your children too hard? What are your real motives in doing so?

14. Are you constantly goading your husband on to success? Why is it so important for him to climb higher and higher, earning more and more money? Is it about him? Or about you?

15. How did you respond to the story of the young beauty queen, who really did get the life we all signed up for?

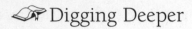 Digging Deeper

✘ Read Isaiah 61:1–4 and 9:
What was Isaiah called to do?

As a follower of Christ, you have the same call. What does God promise to those who fulfill that call?

What does he promise to our descendants?

✘ Read Jeremiah 33:6–9:
What does God promise to do for his people?

What will be the result of God's blessing?

What do you think of verse 9?

Why not turn it into a prayer for your family?

✗ Meditate on Psalm 78:1–8:
What are we to recall?

Who are we to tell?

What will be the results of telling our children about God's faithfulness?

Look up the following passages and note what you discover about children/inheritance:

Psalm 127:3–5

Deuteronomy 6:3–12

Deuteronomy 11:16–21

Deuteronomy 30:19

Joshua 14:9

Isaiah 44:2–5

Isaiah 49:25

Isaiah 59:21

Psalm 25:12–14

Acts 3:25–26

ᯤ Working It Into Your Life

Put together a "Legacy Box" for your children, filling it with tokens of significant spiritual milestones in your life. Be sure to include a letter that explains the significance of each item you place in the box. This will be a long-term project, but you might begin by acquiring a hope chest or something similar and placing a handful of items in it.

If you are part of a study group, bring either the letter or one of the items you plan to leave for your children.

✒ Rewrite This Week's Key Verse

_____

_____

_____

_____

_____

_____

/ Your Prayer in Response

_____

_____

_____

_____

_____

_____

_____

_____

_____

_____

Heavenly Father, I thank you for the gift of my chil-
dren. I know they are my true legacy—the only thing I
will leave behind on this earth when I depart. And I know
that the most valuable inheritance I can leave for them is

a spiritual one. Holy Spirit, I ask you to quicken my spirit whenever I get caught up in the daily grind and start losing sight of what is eternally significant. Help me to focus less on how much my children are accomplishing and more on their heart condition. My family isn't perfect, but they are a blessing. Help me to always remember that. Amen.

CHAPTER TEN

I Signed Up to Make a Difference

Simon, Simon, Satan has asked to sift you as wheat. But I have prayed for you, Simon, that your faith may not fail. And when you have turned back, strengthen your brothers.

LUKE 22:31–32

Unlike so many, we do not peddle the word of God for profit. On the contrary, in Christ we speak before God with sincerity, like men sent from God.

2 CORINTHIANS 2:17

❁Key Points to Remember

✘ One life can make a difference.

✘ The problem with faithfulness is that we're not quite sure how to measure it. We think if we're truly faithful, we will automatically be successful.

✘ Making a difference has nothing to do with success; it has to do with faithfulness.

✘ Many Christians are taught that the only way to make a difference is to "have the life everyone signed up for" so people around us will want to be like us.

✘ When God takes your mess and adds a little age to it, you've got a message! Mess + Age = Message!

✘ We *all* have a message. Some can speak a message of God's abundant blessing. Others can speak a message of God's abundant mercy. The world needs to hear both messages preached loud and clear.

✘ Often, our most powerful opportunities for ministry are borne out of our mistakes, out of our brokenness, out of those things in our lives that we didn't sign up for. Or things we inadvertently signed up for, out of our own foolishness, but now wish we hadn't.

✘ People don't need to see how Christians never have any problems and never make any mistakes; they need to see how God is bigger than our problems and more power-ful than our mistakes.

✘ If we want to make a difference, we will share our lives in a way such that Jesus is lifted up. The punch line of every testimony must be, "But God!"

? Application Questions

1. Do you believe your life has made a difference? In what way?

2. Do you focus more on results . . . or faithfulness?

3. Do you know of someone who demonstrates quiet faithfulness? Someone who will never have a statue erected in his/her honor? Tell about them.

4. Is there someone who has touched your life profoundly, precisely because they weren't successful according to the world's definition yet they persevered anyway?

5. Were you taught that the only way to make a difference as a Christian is to live such a perfect life that people around you want to become like you?

6. Realistically speaking, are you more qualified to speak a message of God's abundant blessing . . . or God's abundant mercy?

7. Are you content with the message God has given you . . . or would you rather have the other? (In other words, some women who've been richly blessed apologize for not having a "testimony," while women with a "testimony" envy the women who were blessed! Crazy, but true!)

8. What areas of brokenness in your life might God be able to transform from a mess into a message?

9. God is calling you to "turn and strengthen your brothers." Ask him to show you who, specifically, you can impart strength to.

10. Which are you more inclined to emphasize: the fact that Christians shouldn't make mistakes . . . or that God is bigger than our mistakes? Try to answer honestly. You might ask your family or the non-Christians in your life what THEY think you emphasize!

11. How much "wax" are you wearing to cover up the cracks in your life?

12. What is one step you can take, right now, to begin removing some of the layers of wax?

13. In your opinion, how do you distinguish between sharing and spilling?

14. Have you been guilty of spilling rather than sharing? In what situations?

Digging Deeper

✗ Read the life of Joseph, from Genesis 30 to 50:
List the broken places in his life.

How did God work through those broken places?

Working It Into Your Life

1. Write out your testimony, without wax. Be prepared to share it with your small group. Pray, asking God to open up other opportunities for you to share, either one-on-one or perhaps in a group setting.

2. Rent the movie *It's a Wonderful Life,* even if it's not Christmastime! Think about the difference one life can make.

Rewrite One of This Week's Key Verses

_____

_____

_____

_____

_____

✏ Your Prayer in Response

_____

_____

_____

_____

_____

_____

_____

_____

_____

_____

Heavenly Father, I am so thankful that one life really can make a difference. Forgive me for those times when I have wanted to shield my heart under layers of wax. Grant me the courage to be sincere. Holy Spirit, I pray that you would open my eyes to see the broken, hurting vessels all around me, and show me how I can comfort them out of the comfort you have given me. I want my life to make a difference. For Jesus' sake, amen.

A Note to Leaders

Dear Leader:

I want to personally thank you for choosing this book as a tool for the spiritual growth of the women God has entrusted to your care. I pray that it will enrich your life as you teach this material to others. This growth guide is designed to make the material as self-taught as possible. When your group gathers, you can simply recap the week's lesson using the Key Points as your outline. Be sure to add your own personal insights and illustrations to bring life to the study.

I would encourage you to "spur" the women on in Scripture memory. I truly believe it is a powerful tool for transforming our minds and, ultimately, our lives. Prior to class, I would encourage you to circle the Application Questions you want to be certain the class discusses as a group. You may not get to every question, but using this approach, you'll be sure to get to the ones you feel are most critical.

I've provided the Digging Deeper section more for personal use. Some women will take the time; others will not. That's fine. I would instruct the women that this section of each chapter is optional and will not be used in class.

By all means, strongly encourage the women to write out their prayers. This is such a wonderful spiritual discipline and may eventually inspire some women to begin keeping a full-fledged prayer journal. Each week, encourage some of the women to read their written prayers aloud to the class.

This can be a tremendous blessing to the entire group.

In addition to the discussion material in the preceding chapters, I have provided suggestions for group activities in the leader's guide section. I would strongly encourage you to READ AHEAD in case there are items the women need to bring to class in order to participate more effectively. Then you can remind them what they'll need for the coming week! Also, you will have to do some advance preparation for each lesson. You might want to just sit down right now, along with your calendar, and note what you will need for each week.

At your first meeting, be sure to emphasize to the group that although this is in many ways an individual journey, you will be taking it together so you can help one another along. It will be helpful for the women to remember that they are surrounded by the "presence of many witnesses" who have walked paths different in context but identical in the concept of conforming us to the image of Christ. Each journey is as significant and distinct as our fingerprints! If you have accepted God's glorious plan of salvation through his Son, Jesus Christ, then all roads lead into the everlasting arms of our heavenly Father.

Women should not compare their life journeys to one another, so as to feel inferior or superior, but rather should rejoice in how far each one has come.

Most people are drawn to a study for a reason. Perhaps they have many unanswered questions as to why certain things have happened in their lives. Others will attend because they have seen friendships tested, often to the break-ing point. Many are living through trials they never would have signed up for. Encourage each woman to share with the group why she has chosen to take this particular class.

This study is an open invitation for us to turn over cir-cumstances we may never have signed up for to God, who can bring something beautiful out of the rubble of our lives. Encourage each woman to affirm her decision, and her commitment to the group, to move forward in search of hope and healing.

Concerning prayer, find out if there are members in your group who may not be accustomed to or who are uncomfortable praying out loud in a group. (Some women have left study groups over this issue.) Make an effort to reassure everyone involved that while everyone is encouraged to pray, no one will be pressured to pray aloud.

Another issue that may arise for some women is hesitation about writing their feelings or circumstances in a book that could be discovered by someone. You might suggest that they use symbols for things they do not want to write out in full. However, be sure to emphasize that it is VERY important for them to write out their answers.

Lastly, ask all of the women to commit to one another that they will respect one another's privacy—that the information shared in the room must stay in the room. Emphasize this as strongly as you know how! If any person's trust is violated, then everyone's trust will be violated and the effectiveness of your group will be greatly diminished.

In closing, I would love to hear from you when your group has completed the study. Please feel free to e-mail me your comments at donnapartow@cox.net. It is my earnest prayer that this study will move everyone who participates in it one step closer to "the life they signed up for"!

His vessel,
Donna Partow
www.becomingavessel.com

Discussion Leader's Guide

Chapter 1: I Didn't Sign Up for This Life!

Discussion

Ask those participating in the study whether they are ready to get real, as it suggests in the first chapter. Ask for suggestions from the group as to what that could mean for all participating in the study.

Suggested Activities

1. Game Show Skit—two contestants answering questions: one always gives the honest answer, the other always gives the correct answer—the purpose of this would be to illustrate the differences in our perspectives and how those perspectives affect our choices and, ultimately, our lives.

2. Take a group photograph and have enough copies made for each member. Ask all the members if they are willing to commit themselves to this journey and to helping their fellow group members along their journey to hope and healing. If they are willing, tell them to affix the photo to the front of their growth guide as a reminder that they have made a real commitment to real people. Talk about the importance of remaining faithful to that commitment even when it's inconvenient, etc.

3. Play Truth or Prayer (instead of Truth or Dare). Take turns sharing one of the top things you didn't sign up for in life. Then spend time in prayer about what others have

shared. After the group has finished the book, come back to the things that were shared the first day and ask everyone how God has changed their perspective.

4. Bring a stack of videos to class, with examples of several different kinds of movies. Lay them out one at a time, illustrating the unrealistic lives people think they can sign up for:

- Action flick: We are powerful. We can "stick it to" the people who deserve it. We finally take charge of things and make the life we want for ourselves. Nothing and nobody will stand in our way. We are in control!

- Romantic chick flick: We have the relationship we've really always deserved, with a knight on a white horse who is perfectly strong and perfectly sensitive.

- Lighthearted comedy: We have an easy life where money is no problem, fun is the goal, and it doesn't matter if our entertainment ends up hurting someone else. We make all sorts of cutting remarks to everyone we don't like, but we are so witty that no one takes offense. Life is a game.

- Intense drama/thriller: People finally see our life for the crisis it is and feel sorry for us accordingly. The world stops for our pain.

- Family movie: We discover that we really were born to wonderful parents and were accidentally switched in the hospital. We are joyfully reunited with the picture-perfect family we've always known we should have had.

Chapter 2: I Didn't Sign Up for a Painful Childhood

Discussion

In the book, I "stepped up to the plate" by allowing readers to glimpse my childhood. Self-disclosure is the hallmark of intimacy. If you disclose truth about your own life, it often opens up others to share as well. Take a poll to see who in the room actually did have the kind of childhood someone would want to sign up for. It can sometimes be helpful to recognize that people who were blessed with solid childhoods still grow up to experience suffering. As the discussions about suffering continue, we need to recognize that just as a rough childhood doesn't mean you are destined to live in tragedy, a great childhood doesn't mean you are destined to a life of ease, either. As parents, we need to provide a solid childhood for our kids *without* sowing in them the lie that this guarantees a perfect life. A solid Christian childhood gives a person the tools to live well in a world that includes enough suffering for all. Are we giving our kids those tools or just a "happy" childhood?

Suggested Activities

1. Recruit two women (in advance) to prepare and act out a "Cannibals at Lunch" skit.

2. Have each woman write a one-page description of her childhood and invite each of them to read it aloud.

3. Invite the ladies (in advance) to bring in pictures of when they were little, and play a game to see if they can guess who is who by the pictures. Then ask each woman to explain how her friends or classmates would have described her back then. How about her family? How did she see herself? How did God see her at that time?

4. Ask the women (in advance) to bring in their high school yearbooks. Invite everyone to share something about that period in her life.

5. Form a Chain of Lies. Bring in black construction paper, cut into strips. Pass the strips out and allow the women to write their "destructive seeds/lies" on strips of paper. (One lie per strip; they can have as many as they need.) Then staple the lies

together to demonstrate how each lie we believe intersects with the lies believed by the women around us. Hang the lies over a cross or place them at the foot of a cross. Alternatively, place all the strips of black paper in a firesafe container, take them outdoors, and burn them.

6. Bring in flower seeds and small planters. Allow the women to plant something beautiful to replace the destructive seeds in their lives.

7. This is the ideal time to establish prayer partners. Phone partnerships are the easiest for most people, since physically getting together can be very difficult. You need to pick a time when you are likely to be uninterrupted (early morning works best for most people) and agree who will place the call. You can pray together daily or weekly on the phone. Praying on the phone is uncomfortable for some people. Explain to the women that they can ease this discomfort by sitting in a quiet environment—perhaps in their prayer rooms—just like they would to pray in person with a friend. Instruct them to limit the amount of time spent talking before praying, since this is the greatest pitfall for most phone prayer partners! Five minutes is long enough to exchange greetings and express specific prayer requests that need explanation. Decide who will pray first and then go for it!

You can draw names out of a hat to set up partnerships or choose another method that works for the women in your group. Prayer partnerships are especially helpful because they naturally roll over into accountability relationships as you follow up with one another on the concerns you've been praying about. Try it, and see if God doesn't richly bless your prayer partnerships!

Chapter 3: I Didn't Sign Up for Disappointing Relationships

Discussion

This week's lesson was, in many ways, the most intensely personal you will encounter throughout the journey. When we speak of agonizing forgiveness, we are getting to the deepest pain a woman can experience. Give the women freedom to share—or not share—who they are struggling to forgive. If anyone had a breakthrough, by all means, let everyone join in the celebration.

Suggested Activity

If you feel the women in your group can handle it, set up a mock courtroom. You will need to assign someone to play the judge and another to stand in the place of the heavenly Father. Let each woman take turns walking up to the judge and presenting her list. (Do not read these aloud.) Then have her turn the list over to her heavenly Father.

Chapter 4: I Didn't Sign Up to Make Foolish Choices

Discussion

Discuss obvious life situations where choices need to be made as well as the logical consequences of those choices: if you don't water a plant, it will die; if you don't grocery shop, you won't have any food to eat; if you don't fill up your gas tank, your car won't run, etc. These simple everyday choices have obvious outcomes. Tie this to the fact that we constantly live with the consequences of our choices, even when the outcome is NOT quite so obvious.

Suggested Activities

1. Remind the women, in advance, to bring in their stuffed sheep. Let each woman talk about her sheep, along

with the "bleating sheep" it represents.

2. Bring in construction paper, scissors, glue, and cotton balls. Let the women make sheep.

3. Do a Window Closing Ceremony in the home (or classroom) where your group meets. Gather by an open window and spend a few moments in individual prayers of confession and repentance.

Chapter 5: I Didn't Sign Up for Disappointment with God

Discussion

Bring a baseball glove to class. Place it on the floor in the middle of the room where everyone can see it. Discuss the difference that would come into our lives if we lived like the glove, moving only in response to the hand of God inside. The glove does not exhaust itself trying to catch balls. It simply moves as the hand inside does, and the success or failure of each attempt belongs to the hand, not the glove, so false guilt is removed. At the same time, the glove needs to be soft and pliable, and it must not slip off the hand or it's useless.

Encourage the women to share which passage of Scripture they chose to meditate on or which member of the Great Hall of Faith they researched more fully.

Suggested Activities

1. Meet in the kitchen, rather than in your usual spot, and make homemade bread (if you have someone experienced enough to lead the exercise!) or simply let the class join in as you load the ingredients into a bread machine. Either way, you can all enjoy the aroma as it bakes and then conclude your session by eating fresh bread. Be sure to bring along some butter or jam! When the bread is ready, place slices of bread on some plates and pieces of chewing gum on

others. Let the women choose which they prefer . . . and ask them to explain their choice.

2. Make a Bible promise book. Have a creative woman in the class bring enough craft supplies, along with a design concept. (You can have all the women pitch in to cover the cost of supplies.) Each member of the class can carefully write her favorite Bible promise in each of the other members' books. If time and space allows and women are so inclined, they can contribute more than one verse to their classmates.

Chapter 6: I Signed Up for Happiness

Discussion

Galatians 6:2–5 says that we should carry one another's burdens but that each one should carry his own load. Explain the difference between an unusual burden that requires help from others to carry and your normal God-assigned load that is your responsibility.

Invite the women to share their lists of the top twenty things they have to be thankful for.

Suggested Activities

1. Perhaps you can find a giant boulder near where your class meets. Stand next to the boulder with a knapsack that has a few small rocks in it. Let the women see the contrast for themselves!

2. If weather permits, go outside and let the women gather a bag full of rocks. (You can supply shopping bags; be sure to double-bag for this!) In advance, assign each woman a specific number of rocks to gather. Next, have the women try to make one another carry their bags of rocks. Talk about whether or not it is fair if one woman gathers ten rocks, then asks another woman who lays hers down to carry her bag.

(You could also have several women prepare this in advance as a skit.)

3. If women have brought in magnifying glasses or fuzzy posters, let them tell the class about these objects. Ask them to share what they tend to magnify.

Chapter 7: I Signed Up for Great Health

Discussion

You (or someone you can talk into it) might come into class with a crutch and a wrap on your foot, a sling on your arm, a bandage on your head, etc. Perhaps several women could put together a skit of people talking to each other about their various ailments and obviously taking great delight in sharing the gory details!

Take an inventory of the class:

✗ Who has a:
  Headache?
  Sore throat?
  Toothache?
  Stomachache?
  Earache?

✗ Who has achy:
  Hands?
  Feet?
  Legs?
  Shoulders?
  Hips?

✗ Who has:
  Itching problems?
  Skin irritations?
  Bowel troubles?

Pray over these areas . . . pray with and for each other.

Suggested Activities

1. In advance, have one of the women prepare a series of stretching exercises for everyone to participate in. You might encourage the women to wear comfortable clothing this week.

2. See if there is any interest in participating in a group fast for the upcoming week. If so, make out a list of specific prayer issues you plan to focus on during the fast.

Chapter 8: I Signed Up for Love

Discussion

Gather the lyrics to several popular love songs. Discuss whether or not they capture the essence of biblical love. If you have access to a cassette or CD player, you might play short segments of various love songs.

Suggested Activity

Conduct the Bucket Surrendering Ceremony.

Chapter 9: I Signed Up for the Perfect Little Family

Discussion

Discuss the type of legacy you want to leave for your family.

Suggested Activity

Invite the women to share items from their "Legacy Boxes." Call several women ahead of time to be sure some are prepared to share.

Chapter 10: I Signed Up to Make a Difference

Discussion

Have several women share their testimonies. You might want to contact several women in advance and ask them if they are willing to share. Encourage them to WRITE IT OUT and time it. (Otherwise five-minute testimonies can last for twenty minutes!) If you really want this exercise to be effective, you might get together with the women beforehand to go over their testimonies.

Suggested Activities

1. If not included in today's schedule, plan a farewell brunch or other special event to conclude the study next week.

2. Discuss what the women would like to do next, as far as Bible study. Perhaps they would be interested in participating in one of my Ten-Week Journey books, such as *Becoming a Vessel God Can Use* or *Walking in Total God-Confidence*. You might want to peruse these books in advance and suggest which one you would like to lead.

3. Conduct the Broken Places Ceremony:

    a.   Prior to class, gather together several lightweight terra-cotta pots, a hammer, a thick freestanding candle, enough tapered candles for each woman in the group to receive one, a match, and several baskets.

    b.   In class, recap the teaching from chapter 10 concerning broken places.

    c.   Place the lighted candle under one of the terra-cotta pots. If you can darken the room, so much the better. (Have a flashlight for the person who will read the Scripture passage.)

    d.   Have someone read selected portions of the passage from Judges 7, where Gideon's soldiers smash their jars of clay.

    e.   Using the hammer, crack the terra-cotta pot just enough for the light to shine through its broken places.

    f.   Next, smash a second terra-cotta pot into enough small pieces for each woman in your group to receive one. (If you have a very large group, you may want to do this in advance.) Place the broken pieces into baskets.

g.　Distribute a broken piece of pottery to each woman.

h.　Now begin to pray, asking God to show women the broken places in their lives. Instruct them to come forward and lay down their broken places on the altar (or at the foot of a cross, whichever you have available in your particular environment).

i.　Play or sing "The Potter's Hand" (from the *Shout to the Lord 2000* CD). If you have a worship leader in your group, please ask her well in advance to be prepared to lead the women in worship with this particular song.

j.　Hand each woman a candle as she surrenders her broken piece, and allow her to light it from the central candle.

k.　Be sure to end the ceremony on a positive note. Women will probably be crying, but they will be good tears. Their broken places are OLD news. Today, you have told them GOOD news: that God can bring something wonderful out of their pain. After allowing ample time for women to reflect on their broken places, invite them to shift their attention away from their own pain. Instead, ask them to envision women in your community who have experienced (or who are currently experiencing) that exact same brokenness. Yet they do not know God; therefore they cannot experience hope and healing. Remind the women that they have an incredible opportunity to participate in God's plan of redemption by reaching out to comfort others with the comfort they themselves have received. Not only can they find hope and healing, God wants to work through their lives to bring hope and healing to others.

l.　Encourage the women to take their candles home and light them from time to time, as a reminder that the purpose of this exercise is not to concentrate on our brokenness but to remind us that God's glory can shine forth through our lives to a darkened world.

1. I Didn't Sign Up for This Life

Deuteronomy 30:19–20

This day I call heaven and earth as witnesses against you that I have set before you life and death, blessings and curses. Now choose life, so that you and your children may live and that you may love the Lord your God, listen to his voice, and hold fast to him.

This Isn't the Life I Signed Up For, Donna Partow

2. I Didn't Sign Up for a Painful Childhood

John 8:44

When he lies, he speaks his native language, for he is a liar and the father of lies.

Galatians 5:15

If you keep on biting and devouring each other, watch out or you will be destroyed by each other.

This Isn't the Life I Signed Up For, Donna Partow

3. I Didn't Sign Up for Disappointing Relationships

Matthew 6:14–15

For if you forgive men when they sin against you, your heavenly Father will also forgive you. But if you do not forgive men their sins, your Father will not forgive your sins.

Hebrews 12:15

See to it that no one misses the grace of God and that no bitter root grows up to cause trouble and defile many.

This Isn't the Life I Signed Up For, Donna Partow

4. I Didn't Sign Up to Make Foolish Choices

Matthew 7:1–2

Do not judge, or you too will be judged. For in the same way you judge others, you will be judged, and with the measure you use, it will be measured to you.

This Isn't the Life I Signed Up For, Donna Partow

5. I Didn't Sign Up for Disappointment With God

2 Peter 1:3–4

His divine power has given us everything we need for life and godliness through our knowledge of him who called us by his own glory and goodness. Through these he has given us his very great and precious promises, so that through them you may participate in the divine nature and escape the corruption in the world caused by evil desires.

This Isn't the Life I Signed Up For, Donna Partow

6. I Signed Up for Happiness

Matthew 11:28–30

Come to me, all you who are weary and burdened, and I will give you rest. Take my yoke upon you and learn from me, for I am gentle and humble in heart, and you will find rest for your souls. For my yoke is easy and my burden is light.

This Isn't the Life I Signed Up For, Donna Partow

1 Peter 2:9–10

But you are a chosen people, a royal priesthood, a holy nation, a people belonging to God, that you may declare the praises of him who called you out of darkness into his wonderful light. Once you were not a people, but now you are the people of God; once you had not received mercy, but now you have received mercy.

This Isn't the Life I Signed Up For, Donna Partow

Ephesians 3:20–21

Now to him who is able to do immeasurably more than all we ask or imagine, according to his power that is at work within us, to him be glory in the church and in Christ Jesus throughout all generations, for ever and ever! Amen.

This Isn't the Life I Signed Up For, Donna Partow

Philippians 2:14–16

Do everything without complaining or arguing, so that you may become blameless and pure, children of God without fault in a crooked and depraved generation, in which you shine like stars in the universe as you hold out the word of life—in order that I may boast on the day of Christ that I did not run or labor for nothing.

This Isn't the Life I Signed Up For, Donna Partow

10. I Signed Up to Make a Difference

Luke 22:31–32

Simon, Simon, Satan has asked to sift you as wheat. But I have prayed for you, Simon, that your faith may not fail. And when you have turned back, strengthen your brothers.

2 Corinthians 2:17

Unlike so many, we do not peddle the word of God for profit. On the contrary, in Christ we speak before God with sincerity, like men sent from God.

This Isn't the Life I Signed Up For, Donna Partow

7. I Signed Up for Great Health

Matthew 9:35

Jesus went through all the towns and villages, teaching in their synagogues, preaching the good news of the kingdom and healing every disease and sickness.

2 Corinthians 7:1

Since we have these promises, dear friends, let us purify ourselves from everything that contaminates body and spirit, perfecting holiness out of reverence for God.

This Isn't the Life I Signed Up For, Donna Partow

9. I Signed Up for the Perfect Little Family

Psalm 112:1–2

Blessed is the [woman] who fears the Lord, who finds great delight in his commands. [Her] children will be mighty in the land; the generation of the upright will be blessed.

This Isn't the Life I Signed Up For, Donna Partow

8. I Signed Up for Love

Psalm 139:13–15

For you created my inmost being; you knit me together in my mother's womb. I praise you because I am fearfully and wonderfully made; your works are wonderful, I know that full well. My frame was not hidden from you when I was made in the secret place. (continued on back)

This Isn't the Life I Signed Up For, Donna Partow

When I was woven together in the depths of the earth,
your eyes saw my unformed body.

Jeremiah 2:13

My people have committed two sins: They have forsaken me, the spring of living water, and have dug their own cisterns, broken cisterns that cannot hold water.

This Isn't the Life I Signed Up For, Donna Partow

AFFIRMATION

Today I will know, firsthand, the love of Christ, which passes knowledge, and I will be filled with the fullness of God. (Ephesians 3:19)

This Isn't the Life I Signed Up For, Donna Partow

AFFIRMATION

I know today will be a great day, because God's mercies are new every morning. (Lamentations 3:23)

This Isn't the Life I Signed Up For, Donna Partow

AFFIRMATION

I'm not going to be afraid of anything today. Because God has not given me a spirit of fear but of love, power, and a sound mind. (2 Timothy 1:7)

This Isn't the Life I Signed Up For, Donna Partow

AFFIRMATION

No weapon that's formed against me today will prosper. All those who rise up against me will fall. Every accusation made against me will be refuted. (Isaiah 54:17)

This Isn't the Life I Signed Up For, Donna Partow

AFFIRMATION

I can either magnify God or magnify my problems. I choose to magnify God. (Psalm 69:30–31)

This Isn't the Life I Signed Up For, Donna Partow

AFFIRMATION

The enemy may come against me one way, but he'll be forced to flee from me seven ways! (Deuteronomy 28:7)

This Isn't the Life I Signed Up For, Donna Partow

AFFIRMATION

I always choose to offer the sacrifice of praise and thanksgiving. (Hebrews 13:15) God inhabits praise. The enemy inhabits negativity. I can choose who I cohabit with. I choose God.

This Isn't the Life I Signed Up For, Donna Partow

AFFIRMATION

I always remember: She who guards her mouth and her tongue keeps herself from trouble. (Proverbs 21:23)

This Isn't the Life I Signed Up For, Donna Partow

AFFIRMATION

I never complain, because it robs me— and everyone around me—of joy. Besides, the world doesn't need any more verbal pollution. (Philippians 2:14)

This Isn't the Life I Signed Up For, Donna Partow

AFFIRMATION

I never complain, because I refuse to whistle for the devil. (Philippians 2:14)

This Isn't the Life I Signed Up For, Donna Partow

AFFIRMATION

I have absolutely no regrets about my life. Everything that's happened to me, even the pain, will be redeemed and turned into something good. (Romans 8:28)

This Isn't the Life I Signed Up For, Donna Partow

AFFIRMATION

This family is blessed when we come in and blessed when we go out. (Deuteronomy 28:6)

This Isn't the Life I Signed Up For, Donna Partow

AFFIRMATION

I am becoming more and more like Jesus all the time: gracious, generous, anointed, and compassionate. I walk moment by moment in the power of the Holy Spirit. (2 Corinthians 3:17–18)

This Isn't the Life I Signed Up For, Donna Partow

AFFIRMATION

If people could sum me up in one word, they would say: gracious. I always extend to others the same grace God has extended to me. (Ephesians 4:29–32)

This Isn't the Life I Signed Up For, Donna Partow

AFFIRMATION

I never curse or condemn anyone, because I want to keep God's blessings flowing into my life. (Luke 6:37)

This Isn't the Life I Signed Up For, Donna Partow

AFFIRMATION

I never judge anyone, because I know everyone is doing the very best they can. (Matthew 7:1)

This Isn't the Life I Signed Up For, Donna Partow

AFFIRMATION

I know that life and death are in the power of the tongue. So I let the words of my mouth and the meditation of my heart be acceptable before God. (Psalm 19:14)

This Isn't the Life I Signed Up For, Donna Partow

AFFIRMATION

I never make excuses for my behavior. All that does is keep me stuck. (1 John 1:8–9)

This Isn't the Life I Signed Up For, Donna Partow